Minister, Heal Thyself

Minister, Heal Thyself

William H. Armstrong

The Pilgrim Press
New York

BV
4011.6
A76
1985
c3

Unless otherwise indicated, the scripture quotations in this
publication are from the *Revised Standard Version of the Bible,*
copyright 1946, 1952 and © 1971, 1973 by the Division of
Christian Education, National Council of Churches, and are
used by permission. The quotation marked NIV is from *Holy
Bible, New International Version,* copyright International Bible
Society 1973, 1978. The quotation marked KJV is from the
King James Version. James M. Barrie, excerpt from "Twelve-
Pound Look" in *Half Hours.* Copyright 1914 Charles Scrib-
ner's Sons; copyright renewed 1942 Cynthia Asquith &
Peter Llewelyn Davies. Reprinted with the permission of
Charles Scribner's Sons. Other acknowledgments appear in
Notes, pages 59–61.

Library of Congress Cataloging in Publication Data

Armstrong, William H. (William Howard), 1932–
  Minister, heal thyself.

  Bibliography: p. 59.
  1. Clergy—Prayer-books and devotions—
English.   I. Title.
BV4011.6.A76   1985   242'.692   85-6465
ISBN 0-8298-0551-6 (pbk.)

The Pilgrim Press, 132 West 31 Street, New York, NY 10001

To

Carl W. Bormuth
and
George W. Webber

and to the memory of

Donald J. Walton
and
Wilmer H. Long,

models of ministry

Contents

Introduction

It should be no secret that the clergy, too, feel pain. Behind the confident appearance of the preacher and the reassuring words of the pastor lie the same agonies that other people know. We, too, panic when we are ill. We, too, are numbed by the deaths of those who are close to us. We, too, know loneliness and guilt and shame. The collar or the robe is no protection from the wounds of life.

Less obvious are the pains and agonies that are peculiar to the ministry: the inward struggle to practice what we preach, the sadness of living too much in the shadow of death, the solemn responsibility of representing God.

We clergy are accustomed to helping others in their pain, but we find it difficult to help ourselves. And if others have not felt our pain, they may find it difficult to help us when we are hurting. These meditations have been written by one who has felt the pain. They are an attempt to draw from the same well we point out to others but from which we may not have

9

learned to draw for ourselves. They are given in the hope that even if we cannot heal ourselves, we may rediscover the One with the power to heal.

The readings and prayers that accompany the meditations have been selected from sources both new and old, for as the older materials make clear, the trials of ministry are nothing new. In the words of the *Book of Common Prayer,* the writings are some that ministers might "read, mark, learn, and inwardly digest."[1]

Loneliness

Ministry is a lonely profession. How alone one feels when standing in the pulpit with scores of eyes looking up, hoping for some reassuring word about life. How lonely we are in the community, having taken stands that seem so right to so few; lonely carrying confidences that we cannot share; lonely behind the unreal expectations imposed on us; lonely after hours, having chosen not to be too close to anyone in our churches so as not to alienate others.

Loneliness is inevitable for anyone who dares to live as a "stranger and pilgrim" in society, and loneliness will be the more profound for one who is set apart for the work of God. But there are resources—antidotes to loneliness—that we often overlook.

The other clergy who are around us can help us in our loneliness, if we will let them. They are probably just as lonely as we are and just as oblivious of our presence as we are of theirs, or just as suspicious of us, or just as jealous. But these are the people who share our work and can understand our pain. If one dares to reach out to them, to drop the professional facade and be oneself, one may find kindred spirits there, waiting to be known. Friendships may be found in the most unlikely places: among liberals and evangelicals; ministers, priests, and rabbis; clergymen and clergywomen; young radicals and tired old drudges. Old fences sometimes hide good neighbors.

Our own parishioners may also be helpful in our loneliness, if we will let them. They may not understand our loneliness any more than we do theirs, but many more of them than we imagine care about us and are willing to minister to us as we to them. If we are constantly on stage, playing the role of minister, they may not be able to reach us. But if we can sometimes be ourselves, allowing others to touch our lives, we may discover the simple human reassurance and support that can restore life's joy.

Although we may be lonely in the ministry, God has not left us alone. Other lonely Christians could be walking beside us. But someone must take the first step to bring us together.

* * *

And behold, there came a voice to him, and said, "What are you doing here, Elijah?" He said, "I have been very jealous for the Lord, the God of hosts; for the people of Israel have forsaken thy covenant, thrown down thy altars, and slain thy prophets with the sword; and I, even I only, am left; and they seek my life, to take it away." And the Lord said to him, "Go, return on your way. . . . I will leave seven thousand in Israel, all the knees that have not bowed to Baal, and every mouth that has not kissed him."

—1 Kings 19:13b–15a, 18

And God stepped out on space,
And he looked around and said:
I'm lonely—
I'll make me a world.[2]

Were you really lonely, God? If you were, then you will understand my loneliness.

Draw me closer to you. Reassure me that no child of yours is ever alone. Then give me the courage to reach out to others, to lower the drawbridge to those who may be lonely too.

Why should we be afraid of one another, since both of us have only God to fear? Why should we think that our brother would not understand us, when we understood very well what was meant when somebody spoke God's comfort or God's admonition to us, perhaps in words that were halting and unskilled? Or do we really think there is a single person in this world who does not need either encouragement or admonition? Why, then, has God bestowed Christian brotherhood upon us?[3]

—Dietrich Bonhoeffer (1906–45),
German Lutheran theologian,
executed for his opposition
to Hitler

Disappointments

We enter the ministry with high ideals and expectations—higher perhaps than those of most people. And that is part of our worth to others, to serve as reminders to them that

> A man's reach should exceed his grasp,
> Or what's a heaven for?[4]

But if our ideals and expectations are high, then our disappointment is bound to be great when they are not met. And disappointments do come. We are disappointed in our congregations, disappointed in our careers, disappointed in our families, disappointed in ourselves, and sometimes even disappointed in the expectations we had of God.

But disappointments can serve the purpose of drawing us closer to the people around us, people who have also known disappointments—sometimes greater than our own. If we have been brought low, others may be better able to hear us when we speak of our ideals, as they might not if we spoke always from a pulpit high and lifted up, from a life free of disappointments and defeats. The discovery that we have feet of clay may open doors for us to others whose feet are also made of clay.

*   *   *

There are shadows of turning on the heart:
   Shadows of advancing age;
   Shadows of missed opportunity;
   Shadows of times when faith and hope
     have failed.
Lord, turn our hearts to thee, in whom
     there is no shadow of turning.
   Renew our spirits when we are weary;
   Help us to see and seize the glory of
     the Now;
   Heal our hurts and the hurts we have
     given others;
   Restore our faith in Thee, knowing
     that "our times are in Thy hand."[5]

—Truman and Virginia Douglass
   Truman Douglass (1901–69), a Congregational
   and United Church of Christ minister,
   was executive vice-president of the

United Church Board for Homeland Ministries.
He and Virginia Zimmerman (1903–82)
were married in 1926.

You must honestly confront your shattered
dream. . . . Almost anything that happens to
us may be woven into the purposes of God. It
may lengthen our cords of sympathy. It may
break our self-centered pride. . . . We must accept finite disappointment, but we must never
lose infinite hope.

> —Martin Luther King Jr. (1929–68),
>   Baptist minister and civil rights leader.
>   King's "I Have a Dream" speech is well
>   known. This passage is from a lesser-known
>   sermon titled "Shattered Dreams."[6]

As spirituals rising out of slavery,
As a cactus blooming in the sand,
As nightingales singing in the darkness,
So in my sadness, God, let me know joy.

Gracious Father of us all, to each of us turn in
tenderest mercy. Our dreams are not all alike,

yet there is no one who has not seen them ground under the heel of circumstance; our hopes have differed and yet each of us has known the futility of a vain struggle to fulfill them; ideals and visions have beckoned to us, yet we have all known failure and shame, and sometimes despair. Heal us, O God, and turn us again, lest we be weary in such labors of the soul. Restore to us the dream and the vision, establish the purpose and far-off goal, make firm as never before the will and its high dedication so that we may lift up our hearts to thee, and cherish thy kingdom in peace. Amen.[7]

—Samuel H. Miller (1900–68),
Baptist minister and dean of
Harvard Divinity School

In thee our fathers trusted;
    they trusted, and thou didst
        deliver them.
To thee they cried, and were saved;
    in thee they trusted, and were not
        disappointed.
                    —Psalm 22:4–5

Rejection

Perhaps it all started in elementary school, where good behavior was rewarded with a gold star. Or it may have been with the advent of the television preachers, so successful and so much admired. For whatever reason, many of us came to believe that entering the ministry would result in winning friends and influencing people. And often it has. But we were not prepared for the rejection that has also come our way. Our ideas have sometimes been ignored, our sermons dismissed with anger or apathy, our vision for society argued down, and we ourselves have been rejected.

How quickly we learn that to follow Christ is to share in Christ's suffering, that we are called to accept the cost as well as the joy of discipleship. In William Penn's words: "No pain, no palm; no thorns, no throne; no gall, no glory; no cross, no crown."[8]

But before we assume the mantle of the martyr, we ought to make sure it is in fact our goodness that people are rejecting and not our pride. Living constantly with the things of God, we sometimes confuse what is ours with what is God's. It may be our own words and schemes, dressed up with divine authority, that people are rejecting, and they would be right in doing so.

When we are opposed it is good to ask ourselves what merit there is in what others are saying, to admit that we are not all-wise or all-knowing, and to join other Christians, both clergy and laity, in the search for God's will. A little humility, a little tentativeness about our ideas will go a long way toward winning acceptance for them when they are good, and will improve our relationships with other Christians when our ideas need to be rejected.

Nevertheless, one prays for strength for the times we are true to God and are still rejected.

* * *

Beloved, do not be surprised at the fiery ordeal
which comes upon you to prove you, as
though something strange were happening to
you. But rejoice in so far as you share Christ's
sufferings, that you may also rejoice and be
glad when his glory is revealed.

—1 Peter 4:12–13

Almighty God, whose most dear Son went not up to joy but first he suffered pain, and entered not into glory before he was crucified; Mercifully grant that we, walking in the way of the cross, may find it none other than the way of life and peace; through the same thy Son Jesus Christ our Lord. Amen.

—*Book of Common Prayer,* Collect for the Monday Before Easter

The Preacher's Mistake

The parish priest
    Of Austerity
Climbed up in a high church steeple
To be nearer God,
So that he might hand
His word down to His people.

When the sun was high,
When the sun was low,
The good man sat unheeding
Sublunary things.
From transcendency
Was he forever reading.

And now and again,
When he heard the creak
Of the weather vane a turning,
He closed his eyes
And said, "Of a truth
From God I now am learning."

And in sermon script
He daily wrote
What he thought was sent from heaven,
And he dropped this down
On his people's heads
Two times one day in seven.

In his age God said—
"Come down and die!"
And he cried out from the steeple,
"Where art thou, Lord?"
And the Lord replied,
"Down here among my people."[9]

—Brewer Mattocks (1841–1934)
A physician and author, Mattocks
was also the son of a Presbyterian
minister.

Failure

The terminology has changed over the years, but the expectation remains the same: that we will succeed in our work. In an earlier day churches expected the clergy to bring about a "harvest of souls." Later it was "an extension of the kingdom of God." Today it is "church growth." And some do succeed in their work, often spectacularly. Churches are filled, and their ministers are honored. But others fail, despite all their efforts.

Those of us who fail may complain that there are other kinds of success, more significant than church growth: the growth of faith and devotion, of service and compassion. But then we would have to admit that success on those terms is even harder to produce and difficult to demonstrate. On those terms even more of us may feel like failures, no matter how great our efforts.

Success and failure, however, may bear little relationship to the efforts of the minister. The seed we sow sometimes falls on stony ground, and there is little to show for our efforts. The seed someone else sows—with no more diligence or wisdom—may fall on good ground and bring forth a hundredfold. If the sowing is well done, there is little to blame on the one hand or to praise on the other. It is God who gives the increase—the growth of the church or the growth of devotion—not we.

We want, of course, to be successful. In our best moments it is to please God; in our worst moments, to add another feather to our cap or another bright page to our résumé. But God neither guarantees us success nor requires it of us. We are asked simply to be faithful in what we do and then to

> Meet with Triumph and Disaster
> And treat those two imposters just the same.[10]

Our real failures show up in the sowing, in our laziness, or contentiousness, or thoughtlessness, or in a harsh and harmful spirit. May God correct our real failings, keep us humble in our successes, and give us understanding for those times when we are faithful in what we do, but without success.

* * *

Sir James M. Barrie's play *The Twelve-Pound Look* includes a conversation between Harry Sims and his ex-wife, Kate, about the reason she had left him.

SIR HARRY. . . . Was anybody getting on better than me, and consequently you?

KATE. Consequently me! Oh, Harry, you and your sublime religion.

SIR HARRY. . . . My religion? I never was one to talk about religion, but—

KATE. Pooh, Harry, you don't even know what your religion was and is and will be till the day of your expensive funeral. . . . One's religion is whatever he is most interested in, and yours is Success. . . . I had to let go; you had only the one quality, Harry, success; you had it so strong that it swallowed all the others. . . . I was even sorry for you, for I saw that you couldn't help yourself. Success is just a fatal gift.[11]

> —Sir James M. Barrie (1860–1937),
> Scottish novelist and playwright

I planted, Apollos watered, but God gave the growth. So neither he who plants nor he who waters is anything, but only God who gives the growth.

> —1 Corinthians 3:6–7

O Lord our God, in whose hands is the issue of all things, who requirest from thy stewards not success, but faithfulness: Give us such faith in thee, and in thy sure purposes, that we measure not our lives by what we have done, or failed to do, but by our obedience to thy will; through Jesus Christ our Lord.[12]

Merciful God, if in the end I fail in my efforts, let me be at least a *faithful failure.*

When It Is Time to Preach and We Have Nothing to Say

The service begins, the text is read—and we have nothing to say. Oh, the words come freely enough, with years of practice, but there is nothing behind them. The faith has worn thin, and the emptiness is showing through.

There seem to be only two alternatives for us and neither of them is satisfactory: to mouth the old familiar words hypocritically or to share our despair with those who are already despairing and who have come looking for a word of hope.

But there is another alternative: to fill the role of an ambassador. Ambassadors do not speak for themselves, but for their countries. Nor is their message their own, but that of another, read out to them on the teletype with the instructions, "This you will say, even to the queen." And they do say it, firmly, boldly, not in their own power, but representing a power far greater than themselves.

We, too, are ambassadors, ambassadors for Christ,

commissioned to bring a message not our own. And strangely, when we venture to speak it, it speaks to us as well. We are strengthened by our own weak voices, warmed by words our own and yet not our own. In preaching we who preach may find our own salvation.

*   *   *

So we are ambassadors for Christ, God making his appeal through us.

—2 Corinthians 5:20a

But we have this treasure in earthen vessels, to show that the transcendent power belongs to God and not to us.

—2 Corinthians 4:7

I was, on Sunday the 5th [of March, 1738], clearly convinced of unbelief; of the want of that faith whereby alone we are saved.

Immediately it struck into my mind, "Leave off preaching. How can you preach to others who have not faith yourself?" I asked [Peter]

Böhler, whether he thought I should leave it off, or not? He answered, "By no means." I asked, "But what can I preach?" He said, "Preach faith till you have it; and then, because you have it, you will preach faith."[13]

> —John Wesley (1703–91), the English founder of Methodism

We are evil, O God, and help us to see it and amend. We are good, and help us to be better. Look down upon thy servants with a patient eye, even as Thou sendest sun and rain; look down, call upon the dry bones, quicken, enliven; re-create in us the soul of service, the spirit of peace; renew in us the sense of joy.[14]

> —Robert Louis Stevenson (1850–94), Scottish author. This is one of the prayers Stevenson wrote for use with his family at Vailima, their home in Samoa.

Troubled About Many Things

Now as they went on their way, he entered a village; and a woman named Martha received him into her house. And she had a sister called Mary, who sat at the Lord's feet and listened to his teaching. But Martha was distracted with much serving; and she went to him and said, "Lord, do you not care that my sister has left me to serve alone? Tell her then to help me." But the Lord answered her, "Martha, Martha, you are anxious and troubled about many things; one thing is needful. Mary has chosen the good portion, which shall not be taken away from her."

—Luke 10:38–42

Some of us always appear to be harried, looking as though we had just learned that our house was burning and we were trying to decide whether to finish the conversation or go home. We are always in a hurry, always preoccupied, always troubled. It is hard to imagine some of us taking the time for a leisurely conversation by the village well or relaxing at the home of friends in Bethany. (And even harder to imagine us daring to admonish our hostess for being "anxious and troubled about many things.")

Poor theology may be at the root of our distress. We assume that God's work depends on a ministry that is in perpetual motion, that attends every meeting and oversees every task. We feel guilty if there is nothing written on the calendar or the phone is not ringing. We doubt that God can hold up the world without our help.

John Milton, frustrated in his work by his blindness, came to believe that

> God doth not need
> Either man's work or his own gifts. Who best
> Bear his mild yoke, they serve him best.[15]

If this is true, what is God's "mild yoke" for us? Simply to be faithful to the people and tasks that fall to us, giving each of them our time and attention as they appear, and depending on God for everything else. With a theology like Milton's, we can afford to relax, to meditate, to give our full attention to those about us, even to "stand and wait"—and in the end we may be more useful as we do.

* * *

Lord our God, Thou knowest our sorrow better
than we know it ourselves. Thou knowest how
easily our fearful soul entangles itself with un-
timely and self-made cares. We pray Thee: Let
us clearly discern their inappropriateness and
scorn them proudly, these busy self-made
cares. But whatever care Thou dost inflict upon
us, let us receive it from Thy hand with humility and give us the strength to bear it.[16]

—Soren Kierkegaard (1813–55),
Danish philosopher and theologian

O Lord, whose way is perfect: Help us, we
pray thee, always to trust in thy goodness; that
walking with thee in faith, and following thee
in all simplicity, we may possess quiet and con-
tented minds, and cast all our care on thee, because thou carest for us; for the sake of Jesus
Christ our Lord.[17]

—Christina Rossetti (1830–94),
English poet

Neglected Families

There is inevitably a conflict between our obligations to our jobs and our obligations to our families. The conflict is greater as we have jobs that are more demanding. And the conflict is greatest when one feels that it is the ruler of the universe to whom one is responsible for one's daily work. How can an elderly parent's appointment with the podiatrist or a child's ball game or a spouse's need for a vacation compete with the demands of the Most High? Is it any wonder that clergy families are so often neglected and resentful?

There are indeed times when the family must take a back seat. Heavy demands are made on the clergy's time, and emergencies arise and must be attended to. But there are other times when we choose poorly, attending meetings that we don't have to attend or making calls that are unnecessary, when we ought to be with our families, strengthening our ties with them. Why do we do it? Is it out of fear of neglecting those who pay our bills? Is it to impress those who can further our careers? Is it because we are drawn to those who idolize and idealize us as our families do not? Is it because we are reluctant to face the disagreements and demands that are part of family living?

At the very least our families should have the same claim on our time that the members of our parish have. If we would drop everything to meet the needs of the parishioner who calls us unexpectedly, we should be equally willing to meet the needs of a child or a spouse, a mother or a brother—or even the friend "that sticketh closer than a brother." But the claim of our families is greater than that. They have a special claim on us just because they are our families, and our parishioners understand that or can be helped to understand it. It is we who need to understand it, to understand that part of our task as ministers is to learn to live in the intimacy of the family, to practice in that demanding setting what we preach about Christian living.

There is something sad about building successful careers in the church and failing in our own families. And there is something good about determining to succeed in our families even if that success precludes what is considered success in the church. For what shall it profit us to gain great careers and lose our families along the way?

* * *

If anyone does not know how to manage his own family, how can he take care of God's church?

—1 Timothy 3:5, NIV

O Lord, we beseech Thee to bless and prosper this Thy household; grant us sweet reasonableness in all our dealings with one another; make us large-hearted in helping and generous in criticizing; keep us from unkind words and from unkind silences. Make us quick to understand the needs and feelings of others; and grant that living in the brightness of Thy presence we may bring sunshine into cloudy places.[18]

—Lucy H.M. Soulsby (1856–1927),
a leader in educational and
religious work among English women

God grant us the wisdom to give our families the attention they deserve, the concern, the patience, and the forbearance that are a pastor's gift, and the love we speak of when we preach. May our ministry prosper in our homes if nowhere else. Amen.

Thorns in Our Sides

Why do we allow ourselves to be so troubled by the difficult people in our churches? God knows the churches have more than their share of them, and they can be troublesome, but why do we allow ourselves, personally, to be so troubled by them? Is it simply because they get in the way of God's work? Or is it because they take too much of our time, or because they challenge our authority, or because they refuse to fawn over us as others do? Is it for God's sake that we resent them or for our own?

And how ought we to deal with them? With experience we develop strategies for such dealings, to avoid being cornered or coerced or blamed, but beyond the strategies, how do we deal with the persons—how do we *regard* them?

With God's help we can learn to regard them as troubled human beings. Inside every difficult person is a troubled human being trying desperately to win attention and love. Going about it in peculiar and perverse ways sometimes, but seeking the regard we all seek. The test of the clergy is whether we can ignore the challenges and affronts to ourselves and continue to treat those who affront and challenge us with kindness and respect.

But what will others say if we do not confront difficult people and put them in their place out of respect for ourselves and our positions? To be sure, others will be watching us. But they are not fools. They know what we are dealing with. They have dealt with the same people themselves. What they are waiting to see is how a representative of God deals with such people. They want to know whether firmness can be combined with respect, whether dignity can be patient and kind, whether love is also for the unlovely. They know we love our friends, but they want to know if we can also love a person like _____.

Among the most difficult people we will encounter in our ministries are our own selves as we struggle to be thoughtful and kind to those who have been neither thoughtful nor kind to us.

* * *

I say to you, Love your enemies and pray for those who persecute you. . . . If you love those who love you, what reward have you? Do not even the tax collectors do the same? And if you salute only your brethren, what more are you doing than others? Do not even the Gentiles do the same?

—Matthew 5:44, 46–47

I am beginning to suspect, God, that *I* have been one of *your* difficult people. In spite of all your patience with me, I have been impatient with others. In spite of your forbearance toward me, I have been unable to bear with _____.

Take away my resentment. Let me harbor no grudges. Give me the grace to treat everyone in my life with respect. Teach me the meaning of unanswered love.

Anger

And the Lord said, "Do you do well to be angry?" . . . And [Jonah] said, "I do well to be angry, angry enough to die."

—Jonah 4:4, 9b

We may be less open about it than Jonah, but a deep current of anger often runs beneath our jovial appearance. More often than not it is anger that we are not appreciated. Our superiors do not seem to care about our efforts; our parishioners do not reward us as we feel they should; and our families may dare even to list our faults. And we are angry, "angry enough to die," when everyone expects jollity or at least contentment.

It would be tempting to express our anger to our superiors or our parishioners if that were not so much like biting the hand that feeds us. We may express it to our families, but they can be expected to absorb only so much. We need a friend, perhaps a spouse, perhaps another minister, perhaps someone completely removed from the church, someone who will hear and accept our anger and then temper it with a perspective different from our own.

We may also, like Job and the psalmist, dare to express our anger to God, who can help us separate the righteous anger from the unrighteous. In honest prayer, life's petty irritations fade away and even real injustices lose their force.

In our friendships and in our prayers we may find that we *are* appreciated, apart from our accomplishments and despite our faults—simply for ourselves. And where appreciation flourishes, anger begins to fade away.

* * *

How long, O Lord? Wilt thou forget me for ever?
How long wilt thou hide thy face from me?
How long must I bear pain in my soul,
    and have sorrow in my heart all the day?
How long shall my enemy be exalted over me?

Consider and answer me, O Lord my God;
    lighten my eyes, lest I sleep the sleep of death;
lest my enemy say, "I have prevailed over him";
    lest my foes rejoice because I am shaken.

But I have trusted in thy steadfast love;
  my heart shall rejoice in thy salvation.
I will sing to the Lord,
  because he has dealt bountifully with me.

—Psalm 13:1–6

Be angry but do not sin; do not let the sun go down on your anger, and give no opportunity to the devil.

—Ephesians 4:26–27

O Lord, help us to be masters of ourselves, that we may be servants of others.[19]

  —Sir Alexander Paterson (1884–1947),
    British commissioner of prisons
    and director of convict prisons.
    He has been called "one of the
    greatest of prison reformers."

Things Undone

We have left undone those things which we
    ought to have done;
And we have done those things which we
    ought not to have done;
And there is no health in us.

           —General Confession,
           Book of Common Prayer

Ministers are by no means free of the sins of com-
mission, but living in the shelter of the ministry, most
of us have been protected from committing the gross-
er sins and from the temptations to commit many of
the lesser sins. It is the sins of *omission* that trouble
our consciences.

There are always things left undone—calls we
didn't make, books we didn't read, sermons for
which we were not prepared, paperwork stuffed in
our desk drawers, people whom we neglected to con-
sole or congratulate or even recognize. Many of us

carry with us a constant burden of guilt over things undone.

The particular things we have left undone may not seem significant in themselves, but they are continual reminders of our failure to live up to the solemn responsibility that ordination placed on us. The ancient words come back to torment us: "The weak you have not strengthened, the sick you have not healed, the crippled you have not bound up, the strayed you have not brought back, the lost you have not sought [Ezek. 34:4]."

Nevertheless, by God's grace we learn to accept the limits of our humanity. We will never be able to do all that needs to be done. We cannot meet the needs of every person in our churches or all the needs of the church as an organization. Nor do we need to. God is quite capable of taking up the slack.

What we do need to do is to be clear about what we can accomplish with the talents that are ours in the time given to us—and then to do *that*.

Some things will still be left undone, undone because of idleness, or procrastination, or indifference, or for fear of the results, or because of some other human frailty. For those things we ask forgiveness and the strength to mend our ways. With God's help our list of things undone will grow shorter and our spirits will be free of a heavy burden.

* * *

O Lord, in Whose hands are life and death, by Whose power I am sustained, and by Whose mercy I am spared, look down upon me with pity. Forgive me, that I have this day neglected the duty which Thou hast assigned to it, and suffered the hours, of which I must give account, to pass away without any endeavour to accomplish Thy Will, or to promote my own salvation. Make me to remember, O God, that every day is Thy gift, and ought to be used according to Thy command. Grant me, therefore, so to repent of my negligence, that I may obtain mercy from Thee, and pass the time which Thou shalt yet allow me, in diligent performance of Thy commands, through Jesus Christ. Amen.[20]

—Samuel Johnson (1709–84),
English author

O Lord our God, even at this moment as we come blundering into Thy presence in prayer, we are haunted by memories of duties unperformed, promptings disobeyed, and beckonings ignored.

Opportunities to be kind knocked on the door of our hearts and went weeping away.

We are ashamed, O Lord, and tired of failure.

If Thou art drawing close to us now, come nearer still, till selfishness is burned out within us and our wills lose all their weakness in union with Thine own. Amen.[21]

> —Peter Marshall (1902–49), chaplain of the United States Senate. This prayer was used at the opening of the session of the Senate held on January 30, 1948.

Grant, we beseech thee, merciful Lord, to thy faithful people pardon and peace, that they may be cleansed from all their sins, and serve thee with a quiet mind; through Jesus Christ our Lord. Amen.

> —*Book of Common Prayer,*
> Collect for the Twenty-first Sunday after Trinity

Doubt

Now the eleven disciples went to Galilee, to
the mountain to which Jesus had directed
them. And when they saw him they worshiped
him; but some doubted.

—Matthew 28:16–17

If even disciples had their doubts, it is not surprising
that we have them too. Some of the doubts are useful;
others can be devastating.

Doubts of the mind can serve us well. Laypersons
are sometimes surprised or offended when we express our doubts about society or the church or the
ways the church's faith has been expressed, but
doubt is the way falsehood and shallow thinking are
exposed. The prophets were doubters of false religion. Their doubts caused misunderstanding too, but
they were the beginning of a more authentic faith for
us all. Doubts like that can serve the church well.

Hard as it may be to accept, a layperson's doubts may also serve the church well. The clergy's ideas need to be challenged too. Sometimes we forget our fallibility and pontificate, dressing ourselves

> in an opinion
> Of wisdom, gravity, profound conceit;
> As who should say, "I am Sir Oracle,
> And when I ope my lips let no dog bark!"[22]

And then the most faithful layperson will be the one who ventures to say to us, "I'm not so sure about that." Doubts of the mind can serve us well.

But then there are doubts of the spirit, those devastating doubts about God's goodness or justice or mercy. Of what use is a minister who doubts God? who doubts that God can "save a wretch like me?" or that God even cares what happens to us? Of little use if the doubt persists. But if by the grace of God we regain our faith, then having doubted can add credence to our message. Like recovering alcoholics who are heard just because they have known what it is to be the victims of alcohol, so ministers who have overcome doubt may be the very ones who will be given a hearing when they speak with those who are doubting.

But if we continue to doubt, what then? With whatever faith we have we will pray that the God who saves by grace will hear the prayers even of those who doubt and will increase our faith until we can once again trust and be useful.

* * *

You tell me, doubt is Devil-born.

I know not: one indeed I knew
   In many a subtle question versed,
   Who touch'd a jarring lyre at first,
But ever strove to make it true;

Perplext in faith, but pure in deeds,
   At last he beat his music out.
   There lives more faith in honest doubt,
Believe me, than in half the creeds.

He fought his doubts and gather'd strength,
   He would not make his judgment blind,
   He faced the spectres of the mind
And laid them; thus he came at length

To find a stronger faith his own. . . .[23]

      —Alfred Lord Tennyson (1809–92),
       English poet

To deny the existence of God may . . . involve less unbelief than the smallest yielding to doubt of His goodness. I say *yielding;* for a man may be haunted with doubts, and only grow thereby in faith. Doubts are the messengers of the Living One to the honest. They are the first knock at our door of things that are not yet, but have to be, understood. . . . Doubt must precede every deeper assurance; for uncertainties are what we first see when we look into a region hitherto unknown, unexplored, unannexed.[24]

> —George Macdonald (1824–1905), Scottish novelist and poet, best known for his Christian allegories and fairy tales

Lord, I believe; help thou mine unbelief.

> —Mark 9:24, KJV

Living in the Valley

Some people live in valleys so deep that the sun sets at four o'clock, valleys where snowstorms can isolate the residents for weeks at a time. The people who live in such valleys have learned to live with darkness and gloom.

Ministers live much of their lives in the valley of the shadow of death. We spend our days in funeral homes and hospitals. We live too much with cancer and heart attacks, with alcoholism and despair. And some days the gloom sets in before four in the afternoon, and we are overwhelmed by it.

How does one learn to live in the valley? Keep your distance emotionally, other professionals tell us, and their advice is good. Find a hobby, others tell us, something that will let a little sunshine into your life. And their advice is good. But pastors are constantly drawn to people who are hurting. We choose not to remain distant, and we carry people's needs with us even in our diversions.

What saves us is the knowledge that none of us is

alone in the valley. The one whom we serve "walked this lonesome valley" too. Just as we attempt to share the suffering of others, the good shepherd shares our suffering. The shepherd's rod and staff are a comfort to us.

The shepherd's cross is a comfort to us too. The Christian message does not gloss over darkness and pain; at its center is the cross. But neither does the message end there. It ends with an empty tomb and an Easter dawn. And the light of that dawn is capable of penetrating the gloom of even the darkest valley.

*　*　*

The people who walked in darkness
    have seen a great light;
those who dwelt in a land of deep darkness,
    on them has light shined.

—Isaiah 9:2

Yea, thou dost light my lamp;
    the Lord my God lightens my darkness.
Yea, by thee I can crush a troop;
    and by my God I can leap over a wall.
This God—his way is perfect;
    the promise of the Lord proves true;
he is a shield for all those who
    take refuge in him.

—Psalm 18:28–30

Give unto us, O Lord our God, the spirit of courage. Let no shadow oppress our spirit, lest our gloom should darken the light by which others have to live. Remove from our inmost souls all fear and distrust, and fill us daily more completely with thy love and power; through our Lord and Saviour Jesus Christ.[25]

Illness and Death

We have learned to answer other people's questions. When at a bedside or a graveside people ask us "Why?" we can produce answers that seem to us to satisfy. But then, unexpectedly, illness and death come to *us,* and we are not satisfied with our own answers.

Why us? Why, when we have left all to follow Christ, when we have devoted our lives to Christian service and there is still so much to be done, why does God allow illness and death to intrude themselves into *our* lives?

We may have been doing what others do, bargaining with God. If I choose the ministry over business, you will protect me, won't you, God? If I put aside my ambitions and continue to serve this difficult and struggling congregation, you will surely bless me, won't you? But God sends the rain on the just and on the unjust; whatever our virtues or our faults, we, too, suffer. There is no deferment for the clergy.

Perhaps there is no deferment because one learns

to minister to grief by grieving, to minister to pain by feeling pain. If there were a deferment for the clergy, we might spend our lives trying to comfort with words that sound no better than a clanging cymbal—and never be aware of it. But if, after struggling with grief and pain ourselves, we can still speak a faithful word, we may be heard.

Here is continuing education for the clergy, in the school of suffering. It is a costly education, but one that can prepare us for ministry in ways that no other school can.

*　*　*

Harriet Beecher Stowe's novel *Oldtown Folks* records a dying man's reaction to a visit from his minister.

> With the quick spiritual instincts of that last dying hour, he had seen into the soul of the [minister],—that there was nothing there for him. Even the gold-headed cane was not the rod and staff for him in the dark valley.
>
> There was, in fact, something in the tranquil, calm, unpathetic nature of that good man, which rendered him peculiarly inapt to enter into the secret chamber of souls that struggle and suffer and doubt. He had a nature so

evenly balanced, his course in life had been so quiet and unruffled, his speculations and doubts had been of so philosophical and tranquil a kind, that he was not in the least fitted to become father confessor to a sick and wounded spirit.[26]

—Harriet Beecher Stowe (1811–96), American author best known for her novel *Uncle Tom's Cabin*. She was also the daughter and sister of prominent Protestant ministers and was married to a seminary professor.

The great illusion of leadership is to think that man can be led out of the desert by someone who has never been there.[27]

—Henri J.M. Nouwen (1932–   ), Catholic priest, teacher, and author

We are afflicted in every way, but not crushed; perplexed, but not driven to despair; persecuted, but not forsaken; struck down, but not destroyed; always carrying in the body the death of Jesus, so that the life of Jesus may also be manifested in our bodies. For while we live we are always being given up to death for Jesus' sake, so that the life of Jesus may be manifested in our mortal flesh. So death is at work in us, but life in you.

—2 Corinthians 4:8–12

I ask of Thee neither health, nor sickness, nor life, nor death, but that Thou wouldst dispose of my health and my sickness, of my life and my death for Thy glory, for my salvation, and for the welfare of the Church and of Thy Saints to whom (I hope through Thy grace) I belong. Thou alone knowest what is meet for me; Thou art the sovereign Master; do as Thou wilt.[28]

—Blaise Pascal (1623–62), French scientist and Christian author

A Fable

It was raining in the forest. It had been raining for days, and all the birds and animals were drenched. The eagle, too, was drenched, and his spirits dampened as well, for his mate lay with a chill, a victim of the constant rain. There was no way to keep her dry, and the eagle looked on with despair as her life slowly drained away. His tears mingled with the rain when she died.

It was raining in the forest. The eagle could not stand the rain. It brought back memories too painful for him to bear. He rose up from the trees, hoping in flight to escape his thoughts. Higher and higher he climbed until finally he broke through the dark clouds into the dazzling sunlight that lay beyond. As the warm sun dried his wings, he suddenly realized that the healing sun had been there all the time his mate had needed it. The pain of knowledge learned too late was more than he could stand, and there were tears for the sun to dry.

It was raining in the forest. It had been raining for

days, and all the birds and animals were drenched. The rabbit, too, was drenched, and her spirits dampened as well, for her child lay with a chill, a victim of the constant rain. She poured out her sad tale to all who would listen, but the other creatures, too, were victims of the rain, and none could help. An eagle happened by, and the rabbit began to tell her tale to him. But she had hardly started speaking when the eagle suddenly lifted the rabbit's dying child onto his wings and began to circle quickly up into the dark and stormy clouds on an errand he did not take time to explain.

* * *

Our pain may teach us how to heal.

Notes

1. *Book of Common Prayer,* Collect for the Second Sunday in Advent.
2. James Weldon Johnson, "The Creation" (stanza 1), *God's Trombones* (New York: Viking Press, 1927).
3. Dietrich Bonhoeffer, quoted in John W. Doberstein (ed.), *Minister's Prayer Book* (Philadelphia: Muhlenberg Press, 1959), p. 337.
4. Robert Browning, *Andrea del Sarto,* lines 97–98.
5. Quoted in Harland G. Lewis, *The Fellowship of Prayer: Lenten Season 1966* (New York: United Church Press, 1965), p. 17.
6. Martin Luther King Jr., *Strength to Love* (New York: Harper & Row, 1963), pp. 78–86.
7. From *Prayers for Daily Use* by Samuel H. Miller. Copyright © 1957 by Samuel H. Miller. (New York: Harper & Row, 1957), p. 76. Reprinted by permission of Harper & Row, Publishers, Inc.
8. Attributed to William Penn, *Penguin Dictionary of Quotations,* ed. J.M. and M.J. Cohen.
9. Brewer Mattocks, *Poems* (St. Paul: The Banning-Johnson Printing Co., 1887), n.p.

10. Rudyard Kipling, "If."

11. See copyright page.

12. Eric Milner-White and G.W. Briggs (compilers), *Daily Prayer* (London: Oxford University Press, 1941), p. 43.

13. John Wesley, *Journal* (London: J.M. Dent & Co., and New York: E.P. Dutton & Co., n.d.), vol. I, p. 84.

14. *Letters and Miscellanies of Robert Louis Stevenson* (New York: Charles Scribner's Sons, 1898), vol. 22, p. 597.

15. John Milton, "On His Blindness."

16. Perry D. LeFevre (ed.), *The Prayers of Kierkegaard* (Chicago and London: The University of Chicago Press, Phoenix Books, 1963), p. 72. Copyright © 1956 by The University of Chicago. All rights reserved. Used by permission.

17. From *Prayers for Every Occasion* (1974) edited by Frank Colquhoun, p. 379; reprinted by permission of Morehouse Barlow Co., Inc.

18. Quoted in Elizabeth Yates (compiler), *Your Prayers and Mine* (Boston: Houghton Mifflin Company, 1954), p. 36.

19. Quoted in Alan Paton, *Instrument of Thy Peace* (New York: Seabury Press, 1968), p. 13.

20. Elton Trueblood (ed.), *Doctor Johnson's Prayers* (London: SCM Press Limited, 1947), pp. 33–34.

21. U.S. Congress, 81st Congress, 1st Session, Senate Document No. 86. Prayers Offered by the Chaplain the Rev. Peter Marshall, D.D. at the Opening

of the Daily Sessions of the Senate of the United States During the Eightieth and Eighty-First Congresses, 1947–1949 (Washington, DC: Government Printing Office, 1949), p. 45.

22. William Shakespeare, *The Merchant of Venice,* I, i, 91–94.

23. Alfred Lord Tennyson, "In Memoriam," 96.

24. C.S. Lewis (ed.), *George Macdonald: An Anthology* (New York: The Macmillan Company, 1948), p. 70.

25. From *Prayers for Every Occasion* (1974) edited by Frank Colquhoun, p. 387. Reprinted by permission of Morehouse-Barlow Co., Inc.

26. Harriet Beecher Stowe, *Oldtown Folks* (Boston and New York: Houghton Mifflin Company, 1869 [1897 and 1911]), pp. 15–16.

27. Henri J.M. Nouwen, *The Wounded Healer: Ministry in Contemporary Society* (Garden City, New York: Image Books, 1979), p. 72.

28. From "Prayer by Pascal Asking God to Use Illnesses to a Good End" in *Great Shorter Works of Pascal* (Philadelphia: The Westminister Press, 1948), p. 227.

About the Author

An ordained minister in the United Church of Christ, William H. Armstrong is held in high regard by his peers as well as by his parishioners. This book reveals the intellectual depth, the spiritual strength, and the quiet self-confidence that make him a person whom clergy and laity seek out for help. He has served two churches during his ministry. From 1957 to 1966 he was pastor of Calvary United Church of Christ in Philadelphia, Pennsylvania; from 1959 to 1965 he also was director of the Philadelphia Cooperative Ministry (UCC), consisting of four inner-city churches. Since 1971 he has been pastor of the Burton Congregational Church (UCC) in Burton, Ohio.

Between his two pastorates he served in the Peace Corps as associate director in Ethiopia (1966–68) and as organizer and director of the Peace Corps in Swaziland (1968–71).

Armstrong is a former moderator of the Western Reserve Association of the Ohio Conference of the United Church of Christ. A native of Louisville,

Ohio, he earned a B.A. degree (Phi Beta Kappa) from Swarthmore (Pennsylvania) College, an M.Div. from Union Theological Seminary in New York City, and an S.T.M. from Lutheran Theological Seminary in Philadelphia.

Armstrong is the author of two biographies: *Organs for America: The Life and Work of David Tannenberg* (University of Pennsylvania Press) and *Warrior in Two Camps: Ely S. Parker, Union General and Seneca Chief* (Syracuse University Press). He has also edited a book for children, *Gerty's Papa's Civil War,* and has contributed the prayers in *Water Bugs and Dragonflies: Explaining Death to Children*—both published by The Pilgrim Press.

He and his wife, Gloria, are the parents of four children.